Th   d
W

S. L. Case

Illustrated by Belinda Swanson

Bell & Hyman

London

Published in 1983 by BELL & HYMAN LIMITED
Denmark House, 37–39 Queen Elizabeth Street, London SE1 2QB

First published in 1976 by Evans Brothers Limited
Reprinted 1977, 1979, 1980, 1983

Acknowledgements
Camera Press p. 38
The Imperial War Museum pp. 6, 9, 10, 11, 12, 13 (top),
    14, 16, 18, 22, 23, 24, 25, 26 (top), 29, 30, 33, 34 (left),
    34 (right), 37, 40, 43, 44, 46, 47
Paul Popper p. 21
The Radio Times Hulton Picture Library pp. 8, 13
(bottom), 26 (bottom), 27, 35, 45

ISBN 0 7135 1483 3

Filmset and printed by
BAS Printers Limited, Over Wallop, Hampshire

Contents

Time Chart

Year	Month	Date	Event
1939	September	1	Germany invaded Poland
		3	Britain and France declared war on Germany
	December	13	Battle of the river Plate
1940	April	9	Germany invaded Denmark and Norway
	May	10	Germany invaded Holland and Belgium and began offensive against British and French armies; Churchill became Britain's Prime Minister
	June	4	Dunkirk evacuation completed
		10	Italy entered the war
		14	Fall of Paris
		22	Surrender of France
	Aug–Sep		Battle of Britain
	October	28	Italy invaded Greece
	November	13	British attack on Italian fleet at Taranto
		20	Hungary joined war on the side of Germany
		23	Rumania joined war on the side of Germany
1941	Jan–Feb		British victories against the Italians in N. Africa
	March	1	Bulgaria joined war on the side of Germany
		30	British naval success at Cape Matapan
	April	6	Germans invaded Yugoslavia and Greece; British completed liberation of Abyssinia from the Italians
	May	27	German battleship *Bismarck* sunk
	June	22	Hitler invaded Russia
	December	5	German advance halted near Moscow
		7	Pearl Harbor; America entered the war
		10	*Prince of Wales* and *Repulse* sunk off Malaya
		11	Germany and Italy declared war on U.S.
		25	Fall of Hong Kong to Japanese
1942	January	21	Japanese invasion of Burma
	February	15	Fall of Singapore to Japanese
	May	7	Battle of the Coral Sea
		27	Japanese conquest of Burma completed
	June	4	Battle of Midway
		30	Rommel's advance into Egypt stopped at El Alamein

	August	22	Start of Stalingrad offensive
	October	23	Montgomery attacked German *Afrika Korps* at El Alamein
	November	3	Rommel's retreat began
		8	Allied landings in French North Africa
1943	February	2	Germans surrendered at Stalingrad
	May	12	German and Italian forces in Tunis surrendered
	July	10	Allies invaded Sicily
		25	The fall of Mussolini
	September	2	Italian surrender signed
		3	Allies invaded Italy
1944	January	22	Allied landings at Anzio
	June	4	Allies entered Rome
		6	D-Day landings in Normandy
		13	V.1 attacks on London began
		27	Cherbourg captured by the Allies
	July	9	Fall of Caen; breakout from Normandy
		20	Bomb Plot—attempt on Hitler's life
	August	24	Rumania surrendered to the Russians
		25	Paris liberated
	September	8	Bulgaria surrendered to the Russians; V.2 attacks on London began
	October	21–22	Battle of Leyte Gulf
1945	March	7	Americans crossed the Rhine at Remagen
		17	Americans occupied Iwo Jima
	April	12	Death of President Roosevelt
		25	Russians surrounded Berlin
		28	Mussolini murdered
		29	German forces in Italy surrendered
		30	Suicide of Hitler
	May	2	Russians captured Berlin
		3	British troops entered Rangoon
		5	German surrender
		8	V.E. Day; end of war in Europe
	June	21	Okinawa occupied by Americans
	August	6	Atomic bomb dropped on Hiroshima
		9	Atomic bomb dropped on Nagasaki
	September	2	Japanese surrender; end of Second World War

Chapter 1 The Road to War

Hitler receives an ovation after the 'peaceful' occupation of Austria

In 1933 Adolf Hitler became the leader of Germany. He was voted into power by thousands of Germans who believed that he and the Nazi Party, which he had been building up since 1920, would end unemployment and create a prosperous and powerful Germany.

Hitler was an ambitious man. He intended to satisfy the hopes of his followers and, in addition, dreamed of establishing a new German Empire in Europe, called the Third Reich, which he later boasted would last for a thousand years. With this object in mind, Hitler began to build up the strength of his armed forces almost from the very moment he took power. By 1938 he was ready to turn on his neighbours.

Hitler's first victim was German-speaking Austria, where he himself had been born. This once-proud nation of six million people had been independent for centuries. In March 1938 the Germans invaded and took it over, encountering no armed resistance. In September of the same year Germany also occupied the German-speaking part of Czechoslovakia, called the Sudetenland. In the spring of 1939, despite his promises not to do so, Hitler took control of the rest of Czechoslovakia and then, in September 1939, he turned eastwards and invaded Poland. The foundations of Hitler's new German Empire, or Third Reich, had now been well and truly laid.

Naturally the other European countries, particularly Britain and France, watched Hitler's progress with mounting alarm. At first, in the hope of avoiding war, they had been ready to accept Hitler's claim that he only wanted to unite the German-speaking peoples of Europe in his new empire, but when he included the Czechs and the Poles, they knew the time had come to fight.

On September 3rd 1939, two days after the Germans invaded Poland, Britain and France declared war on Germany. The Second World War, which was to last for almost six years, had begun.

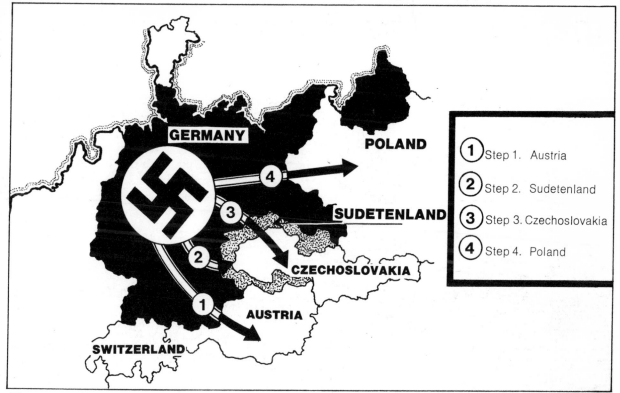

The steps to war

1. Answer these questions in your own words.

What was Hitler's chief ambition?

Which countries and areas did he occupy or invade?

What did he call his new empire?

When did Britain and France declare war on Hitler's Germany?

Britain and France have sometimes been criticised for not going to war sooner. It has been suggested, for example, that if they had attacked Hitler in 1936 before his army became strong, his ambitions could have been checked quite easily and all the bloodshed which was the result of leaving the decision to fight until 1939 could have been avoided. In fact, this was really out of the question. Hardly anyone in Britain or France wanted a war because they remembered all too clearly the horrors of the previous one in 1914, and they would not have supported their political leaders if they had chosen to fight any earlier.

However, when Hitler broke his promise not to invade Czechoslovakia and took over what remained of that country in March 1939, this brought about a dramatic change in public opinion. It was then that the British and French governments began to make serious preparations for war by spending more money on the armed forces, and it was then that they were able to give to Poland the guarantee of help, if she was attacked by Germany, which was the final cause of the outbreak of war in September 1939.

2. Answer these questions in your own words.

Why did most people in Britain and France hope to avoid war with Germany?

What action by Hitler made them change their minds?

To which country did the British and French give a guarantee of help in the event of a German invasion?

3. Draw or trace the map at the top of the page in your book and then write a sentence to explain each step.

4. Use your school library to find out the names of the leading Nazis who, together with Hitler, helped to bring about the Second World War.

Chapter 2 *Blitzkrieg*

German tanks and infantry on manoeuvres

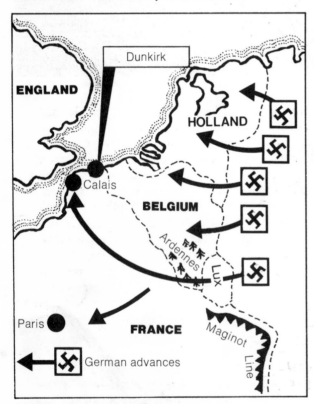

The German attack on France

through the enemy lines, cutting the opposing forces into separate groups which could be dealt with later by follow-up infantry.

With an out-of-date army that still relied heavily on cavalry, the Poles had no answer to this new type of tank warfare. The fast, up-to-date German machines soon had them reeling back, and within a matter of weeks all Polish resistance was crushed. Hitler was then ready to turn his attention to the west.

After its triumph in Poland, the German army was given a few months to rest and refit and then, in the spring of 1940, Hitler launched his attack in the west. In April, Norway and Denmark were overrun and on May 10th 1940 the German army began to advance into Holland, Belgium and France. The Dutch and Belgians were speedily defeated and even France, who was still regarded as a powerful military nation, found herself helpless in the face of the *blitzkrieg*. By the end of May the French army was in retreat and in June Paris fell to the Germans. In a few weeks, Hitler had succeeded in doing what the Kaiser had failed to do in four and a half years in the First World War.

1. Answer these questions in your own words.

What does the word *blitzkrieg* mean?

Which country was the first to face this new method of warfare?

How did the *blitzkrieg* work?

For how long did the Poles manage to resist?

Which countries did Hitler take over in April 1940?

Which countries did he attack on May 10th 1940?

Which city fell to the Germans in June 1940?

2. The main weapons used in Hitler's 'blitzkrieg' attacks in 1940 were fast, modern tanks. Try to find out the names of the tanks the Germans used at that time and the names of some of the great tank commanders who led them in battle.

When the Germans invaded Poland in September 1939, they unleashed on that unfortunate country a new method of warfare. This was the 'lightning war' or *blitzkrieg* in which strong, highly mobile, armoured units called *Panzers* advanced rapidly

The evacuation from Dunkirk (painting)

The rapid defeat of France in 1940 came as a great shock to many people. One of the chief reasons for this defeat was the confidence which the French had placed in the Maginot Line. This was a long series of concrete fortifications running down their eastern border with Germany. Believing that an attack would come in that region, and certain that the Maginot Line would stop it when it came, the French generals were totally unprepared for what actually happened.

Instead of striking at France across the border protected by the Maginot Line, the Germans attacked through the forested, hilly areas of southern Belgium called the Ardennes. This took them round the end of the Maginot Line and enabled them to punch a hole in the French defences at a very weak point. The French never recovered from this blow. Their army was split in two, and the Panzers were soon racing towards Calais and the coast of the English Channel.

At the start of the war, the British Expeditionary Force (B.E.F.) had been sent across the Channel to assist France and Belgium in the event of a German attack. However, when the attack came, the B.E.F. soon found itself in trouble. Forced out of Belgium by the German advance, the British troops had to fight a desperate rearguard action in France to avoid being completely wiped out. Most of the troops fell back on Dunkirk and between May 29th and June 4th the bulk of them were evacuated, either by the Royal Navy or by the thousands of little ships which crossed the Channel to help in the rescue operation. It was touch and go, however, and, although the Dunkirk evacuation saved the men, the B.E.F. lost all its heavy equipment to the Germans. The battle-hardened soldiers rescued at Dunkirk formed the basis of the British army which was able to hit back at Hitler in later years.

3. Draw the map on the opposite page in your book and tell the story of the German attack on France in your own words.

4. Try to find out some more of the story of the evacuation from Dunkirk in the reference books in your school library. Why do you think some people at the time called it a miracle?

Chapter 3 The Battle of Britain

Scramble! R.A.F. pilots rush to take off

After Dunkirk, with France, Belgium and Holland already in his hands, it was obvious that Hitler's next target would be Britain. The expected attack was not long in coming. In August 1940 the Germans launched a furious air offensive against Britain which lasted for several weeks, as Hitler sought to destroy the R.A.F. and gain control of the skies over the English Channel. Once he had this control he planned to send his troops across to invade the south coast of England. They would be transported in hundreds of barges which he was collecting in the ports of Belgium and northern France.

The R.A.F. had only about half the number of planes that Hitler had, with which to meet the German air attacks, and it was a very closely-fought contest. Day after day waves of German bombers appeared over London and the airfields in the south of England and were met by the R.A.F. Spitfires and Hurricanes which engaged them in fierce 'dog-fights'. The battle raged on through August and September, reaching its peak on September 15th 1940 with a huge German raid on London which was beaten back with very heavy losses.

This really marked the end of the Battle of Britain and of Hitler's attempt to gain mastery of the air. Although the night raids on London continued for many months, the big daylight raids came to an end. So, too, did Hitler's plans for an invasion. Operation Sea-Lion, the code name for the attack on the south coast, was called off, and the barge fleets in the French and Belgian ports were dispersed. Thanks to the R.A.F. Britain had been spared the horrors of a *blitzkrieg*.

1. Write a paragraph in your own words about the Battle of Britain and mention these things:

Why Hitler launched the air attacks.

What he planned to do if they were successful.

The code name for his plan.

The names of the British fighter aircraft used by the R.A.F.

The turning-point in the battle on September 15th 1940.

The result of the R.A.F. victory.

The R.A.F. won the Battle of Britain for a number of reasons. To begin with, in the Hurricane and the Spitfire they had two excellent fighters which had the edge over most of the German planes used by the *Luftwaffe*, the German airforce. In addition, they had a very highly trained and efficient team of fighter pilots who fought with amazing bravery in the battle.

When the fighting was at its height, these men practically lived in their machines, landing only for as long as it took to refuel and take on more ammunition, before taking off again to continue the fight. Once the Germans were beaten off and the all-clear had sounded, they rested in full flying clothes ready to 'scramble' at a moment's notice when the airfield siren announced the approach of a fresh wave of German aircraft.

When the Battle of Britain was over, the wartime Prime Minister, Winston Churchill, paid his own special tribute to the pilots with the words, 'Never in the field of human conflict was so much owed by so many to so few.'

2. Douglas Bader, the legless fighter ace, was one of the most famous of the Battle of Britain pilots. See if you can find some more information about him and the other men who flew the Spitfires and Hurricanes so successfully in 1940.

3. Plastic kits of the Battle of Britain aircraft are obtainable at most model shops. Perhaps you and your friends could build some of these and put on a display at school about the Battle of Britain.

One further reason for the R.A.F.'s success in the Battle of Britain was radar. This device, used for spotting enemy planes long before they crossed the English coast, had been developed secretly in Britain before the war started, and it proved to be of enormous value. Radio waves sent out from a transmitter 'bounced' back from objects they encountered, such as German aircraft, and the returning signal could be picked up and accurately plotted. As a result, the Controller at Fighter Command could guess the destination of German bombers long before they arrived over their target, and send up the Hurricanes and Spitfires in good time to intercept them.

Sir Douglas Bader

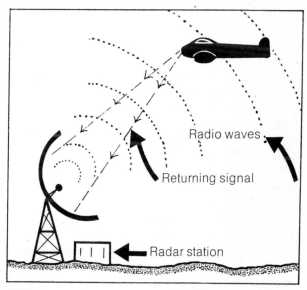

Radio waves

Returning signal

Radar station

Radar

4. Draw the diagram of radar which you can see above and say why it was so important at the time of the Battle of Britain. Try to find out who invented radar.

Chapter 4 The Blitz

The effects of the Blitz

When it was obvious that the Battle of Britain was lost and that Operation Sea-Lion would have to be called off, the *Luftwaffe* changed its tactics. The daylight bombing raids were abandoned in favour of terror raids on the main English cities at night. Hitler hoped that these raids would break the will of the British civilian population and cause them to call upon their leaders to make peace with Germany. These raids, which lasted from September 1940 until the early summer of 1941, are usually known as the Blitz.

People in Britain withstood the terror attacks amazingly well. Air-raid shelters were put up in city streets, and the government supplied thousands of Anderson shelters for people to put in their gardens. Londoners found safety by sleeping every night on the platforms of the underground railway stations, while other people simply moved their bedding under the stairs in their own houses, where they were relatively well protected from all but a direct hit.

Each night the wailing of the air-raid siren announced the approach of the German bombers and ensured that most people had time to take cover before the raid actually started. The night was then spent in whatever form of shelter people had, until, near dawn, the all-clear sounded and it was possible to return home.

In this way, daily life continued. After a night in the air-raid shelter, men went off to work and children to school, and housewives went about the routine business of preparing food and doing the housework. There was very little panic, and certainly no sign that people wanted to give in. In fact, although the bombs caused many deaths as well as terrible damage of the sort you can see in the photograph at the top of this page, they never succeeded in breaking civilian morale. If anything, they had the opposite effect and made everyone more determined than ever to resist Hitler to the very end.

1. Answer these questions.

Where do you think the word Blitz came from?

How long did the Blitz last?

How did people find protection from the bombs?

What signalled the beginning and the end of an air-raid?

The Government did its best to counter the effects of the Blitz. At the very beginning of the war thousands of city children were sent off as 'evacuees' to the safety of the countryside; often to new and very different surroundings and homes from those they had known in the slum areas of the large towns. Their teachers went with them to help in the difficult task of settling them in. Many of the evacuees were treated with great kindness by the country people who threw their homes open to them.

Steps were also taken to improve air defences around the big industrial towns and the ports. The number of anti-aircraft guns and searchlight batteries was added to, and the strength of the night fighter squadrons was increased. They now began to fly the new Boulton-Paul Defiant which was specially designed to seek out and destroy the German bombers at night.

The Government also introduced a number of organisations such as the Air Raid Precautions (A.R.P.) and the Auxiliary Fire Service (A.F.S.), to cope with the problems caused by the air-raids on the ground. The A.R.P. was responsible for air-raid precautions, and its white-helmeted wardens were sent out in the streets during a raid enforcing the rigid 'blackout' imposed at that time and helping with first-aid and rescue work.

The A.F.S. was a volunteer service of amateur fire-fighters who worked alongside the regular Fire Service and helped to deal with the huge fires which were started by the German incendiary bombs. These two organisations and others, like the ambulance drivers, the St John's Ambulance Brigade, the Red Cross and the Women's Voluntary Service (about which we shall read more later), played a very important part in dealing with the many problems caused by the Blitz.

Londoners sheltering in the Underground

2. See if you can find out some more information about the following and then write a few sentences about each.

Evacuees

Air Raid Wardens

The Auxiliary Fire Service

Night-fighters

Anti-aircraft guns

Searchlight batteries

Incendiary bombs

The A.R.P. badge

3. Copy the picture of the A.R.P. badge, above, into your book to illustrate your work on the Blitz.

Chapter 5 Operation Barbarossa

Russian infantry

based on a three-pronged attack. One German army in the north was to push towards Leningrad. A second army in the centre was to strike towards Moscow, the Russian capital. The third army in the south was to advance into the rich wheatlands of the Ukraine.

These armies were three million strong and were well equipped with new tanks and weapons of every kind. Hitler was confident that once his fast-moving Panzer units swept into action Russia would crumble in exactly the same way as Poland and France had done in earlier campaigns. The huge forces were assembled in great secrecy, and when the invasion was launched on June 22nd the Russians were caught completely off guard.

1. Answer these questions in your own words.

What was Hitler's code name for the attack on Russia?

When did he start to plan the invasion?

What was Hitler's object in planning the Barbarossa campaign?

In which three directions did the German generals intend to launch their forces?

Why was Hitler confident that the attack would succeed?

Were the Russian forces prepared for the invasion when it came?

2. Draw the map of Operation Barbarossa in your book.

On June 22nd 1941 German forces crossed the Russian frontier and began to fight their way into Soviet territory. Operation Barbarossa, Hitler's code name for the attack on Russia, had begun.

Hitler started to plan this invasion as soon as Operation Sea-Lion had been called off. The object of Barbarossa was the defeat of the Soviet Union, after which Hitler intended to force Stalin, the Russian leader, to hand over vast areas of territory which could be used as *lebensraum*, or 'living space', for German settlers. In these territories, the Germans were to be the master race and the Russians were to be slave-workers, growing grain and working the industries for the benefit of Germany.

Hitlers and his generals had worked out a detailed military plan for the defeat of Russia,

At first Barbarossa went well for the Germans. They surprised the Russians, whose airforce was destroyed on the ground in the opening hours of the attack, so that the *Luftwaffe* had complete mastery of the skies over the battlefield. Under this air-cover, the Panzers were able to sweep forward in the way Hitler had expected and the advance was soon proceeding at the rate of 30 kilometres a day.

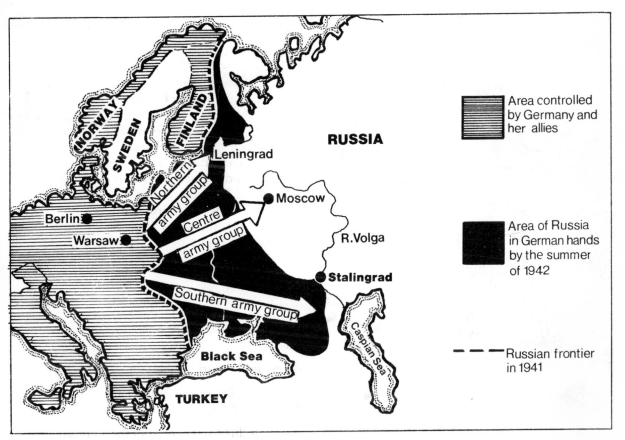

Operation Barbarossa

The army in the north reached and cut off Leningrad in early September. In the centre, the key town of Smolensk was captured, which opened the road to Moscow. The army in the south advanced rapidly into the Ukraine and, in late September, overran Kiev, the capital of that region. In the struggle for the city, 500,000 Russian soldiers were killed or captured.

After these early triumphs, however, the German advance began to slow down. The Russians recovered from their surprise and fiercely resisted the invaders on every front. Then the hard Russian winter began to close in and halted the German onslaught altogether. The German troops, who still wore their summer uniforms, suffered terribly from the cold.

They faced other difficulties, too. Transport could hardly move over the bad Russian roads, and food and supplies became hard to obtain. The bad weather grounded the *Luftwaffe* which could not give the usual air support, and engine-oil froze in the tanks and troop carriers, making it almost impossible to move forward.

The Russians, of course, were used to these conditions, and they chose this time to counter-attack. The Germans were stopped short just 40 kilometres from Moscow and forced on to the defensive. At the start of 1942, although large areas of Russia were in German hands, Hitler had not succeeded in obtaining his expected *blitzkrieg* victory. Russia was very far from being defeated.

3. Write an account of the Russian campaign in 1941 in your own words, mentioning in your answer the early German successes and the reasons for the Russian revival. Take your story up to the start of 1942.

Chapter 6 Pearl Harbor

American ships on fire at Pearl Harbor

On December 7th 1941 the Japanese made a surprise attack on Pearl Harbor, the American naval base on the island of Hawaii in the Pacific. Carrier-based Japanese aircraft destroyed a large part of the United States Pacific Fleet in the attack, and from that date onwards the two countries were at war. Hitler widened the scale of the war by bringing Germany into it on Japan's side. As a result of Pearl Harbor, what had been a European war now became a world war.

The Japanese attack was prompted by a desire to build an empire in the Far East. Even before the Second World War started, Japan had occupied Manchuria and invaded China. Now the Japanese leaders decided to take advantage of the fact that countries such as Holland and Britain were busy with their own troubles in Europe to try to occupy their territories in the Pacific.

Since Holland was already under Hitler's control and Britain was fully taken up with the struggle against Hitler, the Japanese knew that the only country which had the power to stop

them taking over British and Dutch possessions like Hong Kong, Singapore and the Dutch East Indies was the United States. For this reason they launched the attack on Pearl Harbor.

1. Answer these questions in your own words.

When did the Japanese attack Pearl Harbor?

Where is Pearl Harbor, and what sort of place was it?

How successful was the Japanese attack?

What did Japan hope to build in the Pacific?

Which countries had Japan taken over before the Second World War started?

Whose territory did Japan hope to gain after Pearl Harbor?

Which was the only country with the power to stop these Japanese ambitions in 1941?

2. Find a map of the Pacific in an atlas and then identify the following places:

Japan, Hawaii, Singapore, Malaya, Burma, Guam, Hong Kong, Philippines, Wake, the Dutch East Indies (now called Indonesia).

With the United States in no position to stop them after the crippling blow to its Pacific Fleet at Pearl Harbor, the Japanese won a rapid series of victories in the Far East. The American island bases of Guam and Wake were overrun, the Philippines, Hong Kong and Malaya were all attacked, and British naval strength in the area was seriously weakened by the sinking of the two capital ships *Prince of Wales* and *Repulse*. On Christmas Day 1941 Hong Kong fell, and within two months of the invasion British troops had been driven from Malaya and forced to take refuge in Singapore.

This great Far Eastern British naval base had been heavily fortified before the war, when £60 million had been spent on its defences. Unfortunately for the British, the money had all been spent on defending the island against an attack from the sea, and the Japanese invasion came in the rear, across the straits separating Singapore from Malaya. After only brief fighting, 70,000 British troops surrendered to a smaller Japanese force on February 14th 1942. This was not just a defeat, but a bitter humiliation for Britain, and even perhaps the worst blow to fall on her throughout the whole of the war.

The fall of Singapore was followed by further Japanese successes. They captured the Philippines, despite heroic American resistance, and successfully invaded Burma. The Dutch East Indies were occupied in the spring of 1942. The Rising Sun flag of Japan was now flying all over the Pacific. In a matter of weeks the Japanese had carved out a huge empire for themselves.

3. Draw the map on the right and then tell the story of the Japanese victory in your own words.

The Rising Sun flag

4. Draw the Rising Sun flag of Japan, above. Colour the sun and the stripes in red and leave the background white.

5. Make a list of the territories which Japan took over in the Pacific.

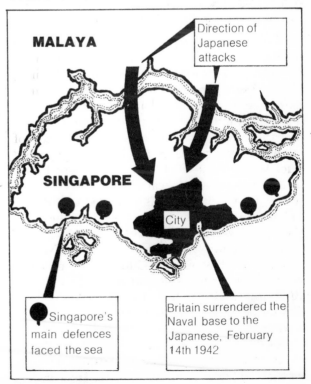

MALAYA

Direction of Japanese attacks

SINGAPORE

City

● Singapore's main defences faced the sea

Britain surrendered the Naval base to the Japanese, February 14th 1942

The fall of Singapore

Chapter 7 The War in the Desert

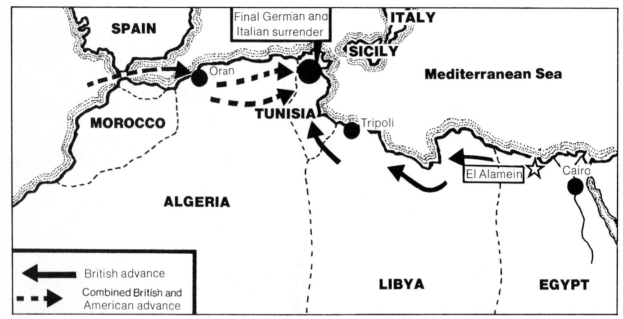

The war in the desert

In June 1940, just before the fall of France, Mussolini brought Italy into the war on Hitler's side. The Italian dictator was not really ready for war, but Hitler's easy successes were beginning to alarm him. He thought that if he did not join his German ally soon, then Italy would not get its share of the spoils.

The entry of Italy into the war posed serious problems for Britain. It meant that her trade route through the Mediterranean was cut. In addition, with colonies in Libya, Eritrea, Somaliland and Abyssinia, the Italians were in a position to threaten British interests in Africa and the Middle East. These interests included Egypt and the Suez Canal, the British bases of Malta, Cyprus and Aden, and areas which were under British control at that time such as Palestine, the Sudan and East Africa.

In fact, Italy did not prove to be as dangerous as the British feared. Although Mussolini wanted war, few of the ordinary Italian people had any enthusiasm for it. As a result, when the fighting actually started, Italy did not do at all well. The Italian invasion of Greece met with humiliating setbacks and small British forces cleared the Italians out of Abyssinia and Eritrea. In addition Italy's navy suffered heavy losses. Part of her fleet was destroyed in Taranto by the British Fleet Air Arm in November 1940, and in March of the following year several Italian cruisers were sunk in an engagement with the Royal Navy off Cape Matapan.

Even in North Africa, where they had made a special effort to launch an attack on the Suez Canal, the Italians were defeated. First of all the Italian troops under Graziani were cleared out of Egypt. Then the British, in a brilliant campaign led by General Wavell, swept into Libya. Almost everywhere it was necessary for the Germans to step in to save their Italian allies from total defeat.

1. Write a paragraph to say why Mussolini joined the war in 1940, and how successful the Italians were.

2. Use an atlas to identify:

Libya, Eritrea, Abyssinia, Egypt, Malta, Cyprus, Aden, Sudan, Greece and Palestine (now Israel).

The Eighth Army at El Alamein (after a freak rainstorm)

The German forces sent out to bolster up the Italians in Libya arrived in February 1941. Under their brilliant leader, General Erwin Rommel, the German *Afrika Korps* succeeded in completely transforming the situation. By the summer of 1942 Rommel had forced the British and Commonwealth troops out of Libya and back into Egyptian territory as far as El Alamein. Here, only about 70 kilometres from Alexandria, the British managed to establish a defensive line to halt the German advance, which had at some stages looked like continuing right to the Suez Canal.

At this point General Montgomery was sent out to Egypt by Winston Churchill to take command of the Eighth Army. A man of great confidence, 'Monty' quickly inspired similar confidence in his men. He began the rapid preparation of his army for a major battle with several weeks of intensive training in desert warfare for his troops. He had large stocks of arms, ammunition and new American tanks to draw on, and was ready to open the Battle of El Alamein on October 23rd 1942.

After a huge bombardment, the tanks and infantry were sent in to begin one of the major battles of the war. The Germans resisted the advance and counter-attacked furiously, and Montgomery needed strong nerves to keep on pressing forward. Rommel's troops fought well in the battle and won many local successes, but by November 4th Rommel knew he was beaten. He could resist no longer, and he ordered his soldiers to retreat. Soon the Germans were streaming back down the coast road towards Tripoli, pursued by the tired but triumphant Eighth Army.

Meanwhile Allied forces under the command of the American General Eisenhower had landed at Oran and other points on the North African coast and were threatening Rommel's army in the rear. Bitter fighting continued in Tunisia into 1943, but there could only be one outcome. In May the German and Italian forces in North Africa surrendered with the loss of a quarter of a million men. Hitler had suffered one of his worst defeats.

3. Draw the map of the North African campaign in your book.

4. Write a paragraph telling the story of the war in the desert in your own words.

Chapter 8 Stalingrad

The Eastern Front 1942

Map labels: RUSSIA; Occupied by Germany in 1941; Occupied by Germany in 1942; Russian counter attack Nov. 1942; Stalingrad; Rostov; Maykop; Black Sea; German advances 1944; Oilfields

The war in the desert, which was Britain's main military effort in 1942, was only a sideshow as far as Hitler was concerned. He was much more interested in resuming the advance in Russia which, as we saw in Chapter 5, came to a halt when the winter weather set in at the end of 1941.

The fighting in Russia flared up again in the spring of 1942 when the Russians made a series of counter-offensives aimed at recovering captured territory. These failed, however, with very heavy losses, and by June the Germans were ready to go over to the offensive themselves.

Hitler decided to concentrate the German effort on one front and on June 28th 1942 he launched a massive attack in southern Russia. His aim was to advance towards the Caucasus Mountains and capture the Russian oil wells in that region. The attack got off to a very good start. The important centres of Rostov and Maykop were overrun and huge areas of southern Russia passed under German control.

In the northern sector of the front round Stalingrad things did not go quite so well, however. The Russians put up a particularly stiff resistance in this area and soon the battle for the control of Stalingrad became the key to the whole campaign, with both sides prepared to throw everything into the fighting.

1. Answer these questions in your own words.

What was Hitler's main military concern in 1942?

When did fighting flare up on the Russian front in 1942?

Which side attacked first?

What was the main objective of the German advance in southern Russia?

Why do you think this objective was chosen?

How successful was the German advance which began on June 28th 1942?

Which town did both sides regard as the key to the whole campaign?

2. Draw the map of the Russian front in 1942 which you can see on this page.

The bitter struggle for the control of Stalingrad began in the autumn of 1942. The Germans found themselves facing the fiercest opposition, as the Russians fought with fierce determination to hold on to the city which bore their leader's name. Every street, every factory and every house became a battleground, and the Germans, who were used to swift tank warfare in open country, now found themselves fighting for days to capture a few hundred square metres of rubble. Their losses were enormous, and one German officer later said that during the battle streets were not measured in metres but in corpses.

Throughout the fighting, shells rained down on the city, lighting fires among the ruined buildings and filling the air with smoke and choking dust. As the weeks passed, conditions inside Stalingrad became so bad that even the scavenging dogs left

German prisoners after the defeat at Stalingrad

the city by trying to swim the river Volga which is two kilometres wide at that point.

The Russians fought the Stalingrad battle very cleverly. While the terrible street fighting was raging and drawing more and more German troops into the city, they began to form a new army group with which to attack the German flanks and rear. This fresh force was ready by November and the counter-attack was launched. Once again, it coincided with the start of the harsh winter weather which favoured the Russians and von Paulus and his Sixth Army, besieging Stalingrad, were surrounded.

Hitler ordered that the *Luftwaffe* should supply the troops trapped in the Russian ring, but in the bad weather this proved an impossible task. The only way out for the Germans would have been for them to turn away from Stalingrad and fight their way out of the Russian trap by moving westwards. Hitler would not hear of this, however, and ordered von Paulus to stand firm.

With suicidal bravery the German troops obeyed this order, but they could not hope to succeed. Running short of food and supplies, crippled by disease and frostbite, the Germans eventually had to give in. Von Paulus and the 90,000 or so survivors of his Sixth Army were captured. The Stalingrad campaign had cost Hitler twenty-two divisions and the German Army never recovered completely from this, its greatest single defeat.

3. Tell the story of the Stalingrad battle in your own words.

4. Here is a picture of the distinctive steel helmet worn by the Red Army in the Second World War. Draw it in your book.

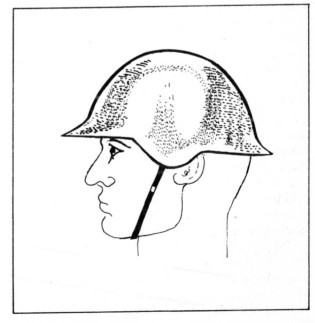

A Red Army helmet

Chapter 9 The War at Sea

The sinking of the 'Graf Spee'

Throughout the Second World War Britain was dependent upon supplies of food, raw materials and military equipment from abroad. It was therefore vital to her that the sea lanes of the world should be open to British shipping.

Naturally, the Germans did all they could to disrupt Britain's foreign trade. One of their methods was to send out fast, modern battleships as commerce raiders to hunt down and sink British merchant vessels. Countering these surface raiders was one of the many tasks which fell to the Royal Navy during the war.

The fight against Hitler's battleships got off to a good start when the *Admiral Graf Spee*, a new and very up-to-date German ship, was caught in the South Atlantic by three British cruisers, H.M.S. *Ajax*, H.M.N.Z.S. *Achilles* and H.M.S. *Exeter*. The *Graf Spee* fled for cover and took refuge in the neutral port of Montevideo on the estuary of the river Plate in Uruguay.

Warships were only allowed to stay in neutral ports for a few days, however. So, after stopping to bury the German sailors who had been killed in the engagement, the *Graf Spee* was forced to put to sea again. Knowing that the Royal Navy ships were waiting for him, and realising that the odds were against him, Captain Langsdorf decided, with Hitler's consent, to scuttle his own

vessel. Pictures of the crippled *Graf Spee* sinking in the Plate Estuary in December 1939 did much to lift the spirits of British people in the first winter of the war.

1. Answer these questions in your own words.

Why did Germany make an all-out effort to destroy British merchant ships?

Which three cruisers tackled the *Graf Spee*?

In which port did the *Graf Spee* take refuge?

Why could she not remain there for very long?

How was the *Graf Spee* finally sunk?

2. Find out what the initials H.M.S. and H.M.N.Z.S. stand for.

3. The 'Graf Spee' was a 'pocket-battleship'. See if you can find out some more about these German vessels and how they came to get their rather unusual name.

After the sinking of the *Graf Spee*, her sister ship, the *Deutschland*, which had been operating in the North Atlantic, hastily returned to port. It was not until October 1940 that another surface raider ventured out to attack the Atlantic trade routes and this time the Germans had much more success. The pocket-battleship *Admiral Scheer* sank sixteen British merchantmen during her five-month cruise.

Probably the most famous German ship at this time was the great battleship *Bismarck*, which sailed in company with the cruiser *Prince Eugen* in May 1941. When intercepted by the battleships H.M.S. *Hood* and H.M.S. *Prince of Wales*, the *Bismarck* sank the *Hood*, damaged the *Prince of Wales* and sailed on, possibly to do untold damage to British merchant shipping making the crossing from America.

The Royal Navy was determined that this should not happen. After the German ship had been brilliantly shadowed by the cruiser H.M.S. *Suffolk*, in order to maintain radar contact, aircraft were called up from the carrier H.M.S.

The 'Bismarck'

Victorious. Their torpedo attacks slightly damaged the *Bismarck* and she began to make for the French port of Brest. *Bismarck* was the fastest battleship afloat at the time. It seemed that she might elude her pursuers, so a 'do or die' torpedo attack by Fairey Swordfish from H.M.S. *Ark Royal* was ordered.

The Swordfish, which attacked in bad light and very bad weather, succeeded in crippling the *Bismarck*'s steering gear and the battleship began to sail in helpless circles. The crew desperately attempted to repair the damaged rudder but they were unable to do so. Finally, the *Bismarck*, still steaming under full power but unable to steer to make an escape, was pounded to pieces by the massed guns of the Home Fleet which had now been able to catch up with her. The *Bismarck* went down fighting, using her guns to the last, and her end aroused admiration among the British sailors whose job it was to destroy her. For the Germans, of course, the loss of this ship on her first voyage was a bitter blow.

4. Tell the story of the sinking of the 'Bismarck' in your own words.

5. Draw the picture of the Fairey Swordfish torpedo plane. See what information you can find about this famous Fleet Air Arm aircraft.

A Fairey Swordfish

Chapter 10 The Battle of the Atlantic

An Atlantic convoy

The German surface raiders never posed a really serious threat to Britain's supplies from overseas. The real danger came from submarine attacks on British shipping, particularly on those vessels bringing vital goods across the North Atlantic from the United States. The bitterly fought contest between the convoys and their escorts and the German U-boats is usually known as the Battle of the Atlantic. It was a battle which Britain had to win.

When the war broke out in 1939 the Germans adopted a 'sink on sight' policy towards any vessel bound for a British port. Within hours of war being declared the passenger liner *Athenia* was torpedoed in the Atlantic by the U30. This sinking was followed by others, as any unescorted ship not sailing in convoy was pounced upon and destroyed.

As soon as they had built sufficient U-boats and had captured new operational bases in Norway and France, the Germans began to attack the convoys. These attacks became increasingly successful when the U-boats began to hunt in 'wolf-packs' of several submarines. These could mount combined attacks on the convoys with so many submarines that the escort vessels could not cope.

In the first half of 1942, 586 ships were sunk by the U-boats and it seemed that Germany was well on the way towards winning the Battle of the Atlantic. For Britain this was one of the most dangerous periods of the war. Its vital lifeline to the United States was being strangled just as it had been in the spring of 1917.

1. Answer these questions in your own words.

Which was the first ship sunk by the U-boats in the Second World War?

What do you understand by the term 'Battle of the Atlantic'?

Why was it necessary for Britain to win that battle?

Why were the U-boats so successful in the first half of 1942?

How many ships did the U-boats sink at that time?

When previously had Britain faced a similar danger?

2. Use a reference book to try to find the names of the main German U-boat bases.

24

In 1917 it was the introduction of convoys which beat the U-boats, and in the Second World War convoys of merchant ships escorted by destroyers and corvettes were again used to counter the German submarines. The U-boats of the Second World War were more sophisticated than those of 1914–18, however, and they were handled with great skill by commanders like the famous U-boat ace Otto Kretschmer, who became a national hero to the Germans. In the Second World War something extra was needed, therefore, if the submarine menace was to be beaten.

Science supplied that 'something extra'. The fitting of improved radar sets to aircraft helped in the hunting down of the U-boats and enabled the Royal Navy destroyers to catch them on the surface at night, when they had come up to recharge their batteries. Asdic, the underwater echo-sounding gear fitted to destroyers and other escort vessels, also helped in the battle. So, too, did the improved and very accurate location equipment which was designed to pick up the U-boats' radio signals. New and more powerful depth-charges were also introduced.

By the use of these aids and of a greater number of escorts and spotter aircraft, the British eventually brought the U-boat threat under control. In March 1943 two convoys were set upon by large wolf-packs and twenty-one ships were lost, but nearly every U-boat was damaged in the process. For the U-boats, the days of easy pickings were over, and by the summer of 1943 the tide had turned and the Battle of the Atlantic was going against the Germans.

The losses of allied shipping went down month by month, and even though the Germans began to use the schnorkel device to recharge their batteries while remaining submerged, which cut their losses, they never regained the upper hand. It had been a close-run thing, but Britain and her allies had finally won the Battle of the Atlantic.

Depth-charging

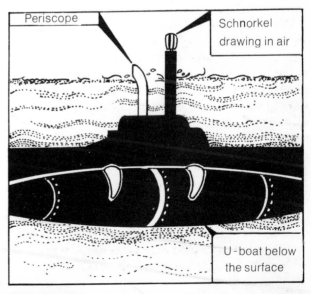

Periscope

Schnorkel drawing in air

U-boat below the surface

The schnorkel

3. How did science enable Britain to win the Battle of the Atlantic?

4. Draw the picture of the schnorkel and try to find out some more about this device.

Chapter 11 The Home Front

You never know who's listening!

CARELESS TALK COSTS LIVES

Everyday life in Britain was greatly affected by the Second World War. The towns took on a new appearance, with black and white painted lamp-posts and kerbs to enable people to avoid them in the blackout, while important public buildings were sandbagged to protect them from bomb damage. Emergency water supply tanks were put up on public squares and patches of waste ground to provide firefighters with a readily available source of water, and private cars almost disappeared from the city streets.

Everywhere there were brick-built air-raid shelters and A.R.P. posts, and most houses had their windows criss-crossed with sticky tape to cut down the danger of flying glass splinters during the air-raids. People in the streets could be seen hurrying along with their gas masks (with which every citizen had been issued before the war actually started) and large numbers of people were in uniform of one sort or another.

Even the advertising hoardings changed their appearance and became covered with wartime notices issued by the Government, urging people to 'Dig for Victory' or reminding them that 'Careless Talk Costs Lives' and that 'Coughs and Sneezes Spread Diseases'. It was impossible to walk any distance down a city street in Britain without being constantly reminded in various different ways that the country was at war.

1. Write a paragraph about some of the ways in which the appearance of our towns was altered by the outbreak of the Second World War.

The war not only affected the appearance of British towns and cities; it also had a very great impact on family life. Thousands of men were called up for active service and their wives and children had to get used to managing without them. The occasional fourteen days' leave, when the men were allowed to come home, was an event that was eagerly looked forward to.

(Above left) A wartime poster
(Below left) Sandbags and painted kerbs in wartime London

Children being evacuated in 1939

Something else which disrupted family life was the evacuation of schoolchildren from the big cities to places of safety in the country. When the Government began this policy of evacuation, two days before the war broke out, it was possible to see long queues of children, each with an identification label, waiting to board the trains at the major railway stations. Worried parents said tearful goodbyes and waited to see the harassed teachers get the children on board the trains to begin their journey into the unknown.

Later in the war, when it became necessary to increase the country's labour force and extend the armed forces, women were called up to go into the services or into war work in one of the big munitions factories. This meant that the older single girls in a family, who were liable for call up, left home. So there was still more disruption to normal family life.

Finally, thousands of families were directly affected by the bombing. In the air-raids, 200,000 houses were totally destroyed and a further three million were damaged. This meant, at the very least, the destruction of furniture and the loss of prized personal possessions, and all the

difficulties of trying to set up a new home at a time when everything from pots and pans to bed linen was in short supply or on ration. There can have been few families in Britain by 1945 who were not affected in some way by the war.

2. Talk to your grandparents and anyone else in your family who can remember the Second World War and find out how they were affected by it.

3. Try to imagine your feelings if you were an evacuee like the ones in the picture at the top of this page, getting ready to depart for your new home in the country. Write down how you think you might feel.

4. Many families suffered hardship in the early part of the war because the allowances made to a serviceman's family were not very generous. Try to find out how much an ordinary private soldier's wife received if she had two children to keep at the start of the war.

Chapter 12 Shortages

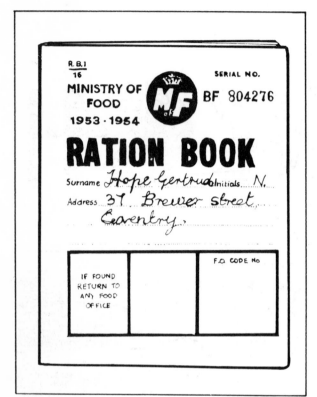

A ration book

One feature of the Second World War which almost everyone who lived through it remembers was rationing. Food rationing began in January 1940 when bacon, sugar and butter first went on coupons. The system was gradually extended in the months that followed, until almost all basic foodstuffs had to be bought on ration. Eventually, most people were permitted an average weekly allowance of 113 grams of bacon, 57 grams of cooking fat, 57 grams of butter, 113 grams of margarine, 57 grams of tea, 140 grams of sugar and 57 grams of cheese.

Meat was also rationed, not by weight, but by price. To begin with, a person's weekly allowance was one shilling and tenpence (8 n.p.) worth per week. Later, when food became even more scarce, the ration was reduced to one shilling and twopence (6 n.p.). Other food items such as jam, syrup, tinned fruit, baked beans, breakfast cereals and biscuits could only be obtained by exchanging points from the ration book for them. The points value of these goods was constantly changing, depending upon the availability of stocks, and so a wartime housewife had to keep her wits about her to make sure that she got the best possible value for her family's points.

To make sure that every citizen got the correct ration of food, the Government issued each person with a ration book. The family then registered with a particular grocer and butcher. The grocers and butchers received enough food to give the correct amount to each of their registered customers.

Ordinary ration books were buff in colour, but there were also green and blue books. The green books were issued to expectant mothers and very young children and entitled them to extra milk and eggs, and special foods such as concentrated orange juice. The blue books were issued to children of school age, who were allowed an extra half pint (quarter litre) of milk a day, and they could occasionally be used to obtain food in very short supply such as bananas.

The whole food rationing system, which was fair and gave everyone a balanced and healthy diet during the war, was brilliantly organised by the Ministry of Food under its head, Lord Woolton.

1. Write a paragraph in your own words about food rationing during the war, saying how the system worked and how much food people were entitled to.

2. Why do you think food rationing was necessary?

Food was not the only commodity in short supply during the war. Sweets, petrol, clothing and even soap went on ration, and many other things were hard to obtain. There was, for example, an almost continual shortage of fuel, and gas and electricity supplies were often cut. Everyday items like cigarettes went 'under the counter' to regular customers only, in most shops, and children grew used to being without metal toys, ice-cream and other things now taken for granted. Grown-ups had to cope with severe shortages of such things as razorblades, matches, crockery and make-up and the virtual disappearance of items like artificial silk stockings.

The Government did its best to eke out what goods were available and one quite successful method which they employed was a deliberate drop in quality. Goods known as 'utility' and bearing the special CC41 mark, which you can see in the diagram, were manufactured to lower standards of finish than in peacetime so as to make what raw materials were available go round a bit further. You can still occasionally see the utility mark on furniture and clothes made during the war, and obtain old books printed on cheap war economy paper.

People coped very well with the shortages. They 'dug for victory' by producing their own vegetables in their gardens or on allotments, and they learned how to improvise. Soya bean flour was used to make marzipan for wartime Christmas cakes and gelatine crystals mixed with 'green book' orange juice made party jellies. When the Government banned cake icing as wasteful of valuable sugar supplies, people even made do with cardboard wedding cakes.

Everyone naturally looked forward to the end of the fighting and a return to normal, but by and large people in Britain accepted the shortages good-humouredly as a very necessary part of the war effort. There were inevitably people who tried to cheat by buying extra goods on the 'black market', but the Government did its best to limit the amount of unfair trade and the public generally backed them up in their efforts.

3. Draw the utility mark in your book, and write one or two sentences to say what utility goods were.

4. What do you understand by the term 'black market'?

5. Write down one or two of the ways in which people tried to overcome the shortages. See if you can find out any more from members of your family.

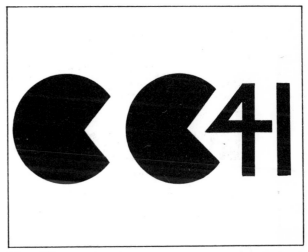

The utility mark

A poster urging people to grow their own food

Chapter 13 Your Country Needs You

The whole of the manpower of Britain was organised to fight the Second World War. Men between the ages of eighteen and forty-five were called up for military service, unless they were medically unfit or in some vital civilian job.

These 'reserved occupations', as they were called, included such things as farm work and coal mining, and important industrial jobs such as ship-building. Coal production was, of course, very important to the war effort, and some of the men who were called up, expecting to serve in the forces, found themselves drafted into the coal mines instead.

After 1941 women were also called up, and many went into the women's services. These were the Auxiliary Territorial Service, or A.T.S., attached to the army, the Women's Auxiliary Air Force, known as the W.A.A.F.s, and the Women's Royal Naval Service, the W.R.N.S. Other girls were sent into the munitions factories and some joined the Women's Land Army and went into farm work.

All these groups did work of great national importance. The women's services released men to serve at the fighting fronts, the Land Army girls helped with the constant battle to overcome the food shortage and the factory girls assisted in keeping up the flow of arms and ammunition. Without the contribution made by women during the war, Britain could not have kept up its war effort.

Organising manpower on the scale on which it was done during the war was a very difficult job, and it was handled with very great skill by Ernest Bevin, the wartime Minister of Labour.

1. Answer these questions in your own words.

Who was called up for military service?

Which groups of men were not required to go?

Which services could women join?

What other work did women do?

How important was the contribution women made to the war effort?

Who organised manpower during the war?

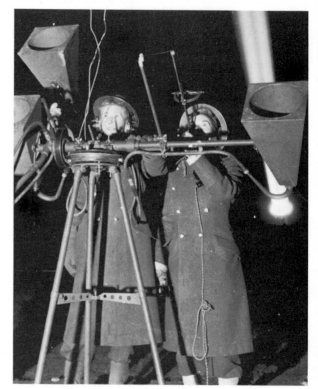

A.T.S. girls manning a sound detector

2. See if you can find out any details about the uniforms worn by the three women's services in the war and the uniforms worn by the Women's Land Army.

One wartime call-up which met with an immediate response was the Government's request for recruits for the Local Defence Volunteers. The appeal for volunteers was broadcast over the radio on Tuesday May 14th 1940, when Hitler's invasion was expected at almost any time and within twenty-four hours 250,000 men between the ages of seventeen and sixty-five had answered the call. They were hastily organised into local units and issued with armbands bearing the letters L.D.V. because there were no uniforms for them. Gunsmiths, shops and museums were ransacked to find arms for them, and when these were not available men went on duty armed with whatever they could find to use as weapons.

Shortly afterwards the L.D.V. changed its name to Home Guard and, later, proper uniforms were issued and the men were provided with rifles and Bren guns and trained how to use them. They became a valuable volunteer reserve army. The fact that they were never called upon to defend their towns and villages, or fire many shots in anger, does not detract from the enthusiasm and patriotism they demonstrated at a time of great national danger.

There were, of course, many other ways in which people could give voluntary, unpaid service to the country during the war. As we have seen already, men became air-raid wardens, firemen and ambulance drivers during the Blitz, and many women acted as nurses and did first-aid. Others joined the W.V.S., the Women's Voluntary Service, which helped in countless ways. W.V.S. ladies manned forces canteens, assisted with the care of bombed-out families after the Blitz, wrapped food parcels for the troops and were on hand with cups of tea and kindly assistance in almost every emergency.

The people in all these organisations gave their time and their energy quite freely and with great enthusiasm because there was a widespread desire to help. People in Britain believed the war was necessary to destroy Hitler and the terrible ideas that he stood for and that it was something to which everybody should contribute.

3. Write a paragraph about the Home Guard and the W.V.S.

4. Copy the picture of the soldier in battledress which you can see on the right. This uniform was issued to both the regular army and the Home Guard.

5. The last few chapters have told you a lot about life in Britain during the war. Many people still have in their homes some of the things which have been mentioned, such as ration books, gas masks and so forth. See if you can make a collection of some of these items and put on a display in your school about life during the war.

A soldier in 1939–45 battledress

Chapter 14 Hitler's Europe

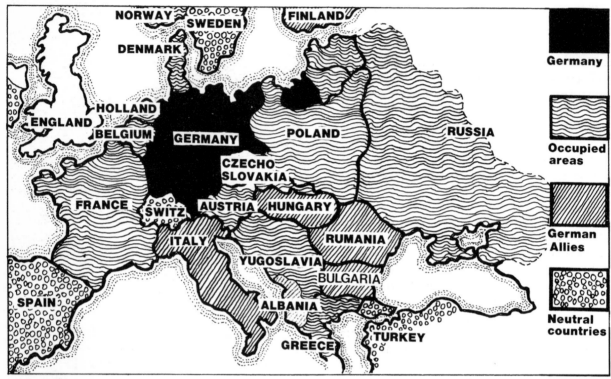

Hitler's Europe

By the end of 1942 Hitler controlled almost the whole of Europe. The area under German domination stretched from the Atlantic coast of France to the heart of Soviet Russia. Many other countries in Europe which had not been conquered were Hitler's allies, while countries like Sweden, Spain, Switzerland and Eire were neutral and played no part in the war. Only Britain in western Europe and Russia in the east remained to oppose the German dictator.

Within the vast area of German-occupied Europe Hitler tried to establish the Nazi 'New Order'. Strict obedience to German wishes was enforced by the *Gestapo* (Hitler's secret police) and the dreaded S.S. The black-uniformed S.S., with their death's head cap badge, had originally been Hitler's personal bodyguard. By the time the war broke out, they had grown into a large formation of fanatical Nazis who were prepared to carry out any order given by the Führer, however cruel or savage it might be. Using these willing servants, Hitler organised the conquered countries to serve German interests.

The western European countries, such as France, Holland and Belgium, and the Scandinavian countries of Norway and Denmark, for which Hitler had some respect, were not treated as harshly as they might have been, although their industries and agriculture were harnessed to the German war effort.

However, in the eastern territories it was a different story. These areas, which were regarded as *lebensraum* or 'living space' for future German settlers, were treated with great severity. Himmler, the leader of the Nazi S.S., gave his men a completely free hand in Poland and Russia and they often behaved inhumanly. Men, women and children were arrested and shot and their homes and belongings were burned to the ground. Thousands of other people were rounded up as forced labourers and sent to work camps or to German factories, where they were treated like slaves. When there was any opposition to this brutal behaviour it was ruthlessly put down.

1. Use the map on the opposite page to answer the following questions:

Which countries had Hitler conquered by the end of 1942?

Which countries were allies of Germany?

Which countries remained neutral?

2. How did the treatment of the conquered countries of western Europe differ from the treatment given to those in the east?

3. See if you can find out any information about the villages of Lidice in Czechoslovakia and Oradour in France and the way they were dealt with by the S.S.

The most horrifying feature of Hitler's rule was his treatment of the Jews. Hitler and most of the other Nazi leaders were anti-Semitic, which means that they hated not just some Jews but all of them, simply because they were Jews. Unfortunately, there have always been people who held these views, and the Jewish race has been persecuted for hundreds of years. However, it was never on the vast, highly organised scale practised by Hitler. His 'Final Solution' to the Jewish problem, as he called it, was the wholesale murder of millions of Jews all over the occupied territories.

The plans first went into operation in 1941 when Russia was invaded. Special Action Units of the S.S. followed the front line troops into Russia and executed more than 100,000 Russian Jews in the first five months of the campaign. In all, nearly one and a half million Jews were killed by the Germans in Russia before the end of the war.

At the end of 1941 the second stage of the 'Final Solution' began, with the deportation of Polish Jews to concentration camps. In 1942 the same policy was applied to the rest of the occupied areas, including those in western Europe. Many of these camps were, in fact, extermination camps where the Jews were taken to be murdered. The first executions took place at Chelmno camp in Poland in March 1942 and after that the programme of executions went on at Auschwitz, Treblinka and many other centres. By the time the first death camps were liberated by the advancing Allied armies in the closing months of the war, six million Jews had died.

Hitler's methods aroused some opposition

Concentration camp victims being buried after the liberation

inside Germany itself where many of the ordinary German people were horrified at his treatment of the Jews. They were also appalled by other crimes carried out on his orders, like the killing of people who were crippled or mentally handicapped or in some other way 'inferior', as far as the Nazi leaders were concerned.

Unfortunately, this opposition was not very widespread, because so many Germans were dazzled by Hitler's military successes. It was only later on in the war, when it became obvious that the Germans were losing, that the opposition reached a point at which one of Hitler's fellow countrymen was prepared to make an attempt on his leader's life. This was in the unsuccessful Bomb Plot of July 1944.

4. Write a paragraph describing Hitler's treatment of the Jews.

5. Try to obtain a copy of 'The Diary of Anne Frank' from a library. In it you will find the moving story of a young Dutch Jewess who hid from the Nazis in occupied Holland.

6. Try to find out some more about the Bomb Plot in 1944.

Chapter 15 The Invasion of Italy

Allied landings on the coast of Italy

As we saw at the end of Chapter 7, the German and Italian forces were finally cleared out of North Africa in May 1943. The British and Americans followed up this success almost immediately, with a landing on the island of Sicily. This invasion met with only limited resistance, and within thirty-eight days Sicily was entirely in Allied hands.

The victory in Sicily had a very important result. When the fighting for the island was at its height, the war-weary Italians turned against Mussolini. He was arrested by his own people and replaced as leader of Italy by Marshal Badoglio, who immediately began secret negotiations with the Allies to arrange an Italian surrender.

Unfortunately, these negotiations took several weeks and Hitler, who realised what was going on, used the time to build up his own forces in the Italian peninsula. As a result, when the new Italian government did surrender officially, early in September 1943, the Allied invasion of Italy, which had been timed to coincide with that surrender, met with very fierce German resistance. Instead of falling easily into Allied hands, as some people had forecast, Italy had to be fought for in a long gruelling campaign which used up Allied resources at a time when they could have been more usefully employed elsewhere.

1. Answer these questions in your own words.

When was Sicily invaded by the Allies?

How long did it take to conquer the island?

What was the important result of the Allied success in Sicily?

Who replaced Mussolini as the new leader of Italy?

What did the long negotiations over the Italian surrender terms allow Hitler to do?

What effect did this have on the Allied plans for capturing Italy?

2. Draw the map of the Italian campaign which you can see below.

From the Allied point of view, the invasion of Italy got off to quite a good start. The landings themselves were a success and, by October 1st 1943, the two important towns of Naples and Foggia in southern Italy were in American and British hands. With the onset of winter and very heavy rains, however, the advance slowed down. The Germans cleverly used the natural obstacles, such as the Italian rivers and mountains, to their advantage and the campaign became a slogging match. The British and Americans were forced to inch their way forward against stiff, well-organised German opposition.

An attempt was made to try to take the Germans in the rear by a landing at Anzio, but this failed through the over-cautious attitude of the commanding general. As a result there were months of bitter fighting round Monte Cassino before the Americans were able to push forward as far as Rome, which fell to them in June 1944. In the winter of the same year the Germans constructed new defensive lines in the north of Italy and held up the Allied advance for a second winter. It was not until the spring of 1945 that Field-Marshal Alexander, the Allied commander, was able to make his final assault and force the surrender of the German forces in Italy on April 29th 1945.

By this time Mussolini was dead. After his arrest in the summer of 1943 by his own followers, he had been imprisoned but was rescued by the German commando leader Otto Skorzeny. Hitler then appointed him the puppet ruler of northern Italy and he continued in some sort of power. In April 1945, however, Italian resistance fighters, who were on the side of the Allies, captured Mussolini as he was trying to escape with his mistress, Clara Petacci, and they were both executed. Their bodies were then taken to Milan where they were hung upside down from a lamp-post to be jeered at by the crowds. That was the end of the once-proud dictator of Italy.

3. Tell the story of the Allied battle for Italy in your own words.

Key

→ Allied advances

▲▲▲ German winter defence lines of 1943 1944

● Towns mentioned in text

Milan

Dec 1944

Dec 1943

Rome

Anzio

Foggia

Cassino

Naples

Unsuccessful Allied landing at Anzio

SICILY

Chapter 16 The Bombers

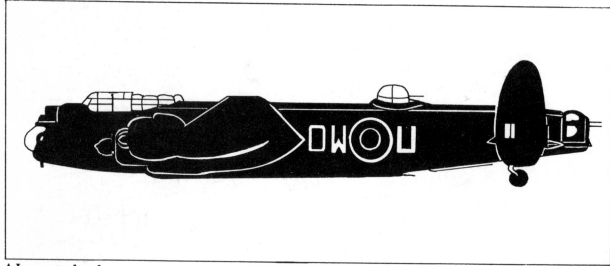

A Lancaster bomber

The Blitz of London in 1940 and 1941 caused considerable damage and loss of life, but it did not compare with the terrible Allied air offensive against Germany. This systematic attempt to destroy Germany's industries and the major German cities began in 1942 and continued with mounting fury until the very end of the war. By that time, Berlin, Hamburg, Cologne and many other German towns lay in ruins, and hundreds of factories and steel mills had been reduced to rubble.

The British and Americans co-operated closely in the bomber campaign, but each developed their own particular method. The Americans, using their heavily armed Flying Fortresses, specialised in high-level precision bombing, in daylight, of selected targets such as factories, and they achieved some spectacular results.

The R.A.F., on the other hand, specialised in the area bombing of German cities at night. The Lancasters, their way lit by Mosquito 'Pathfinders', saturated their targets with such a weight of high explosive and incendiary bombs that they often caused fire-storms. When these occurred, so much oxygen was drawn into the fire that there was not enough left for people to breathe. Civilians who were not killed in this way were often baked alive in the cellars to which they had gone for shelter, while their homes were turned into the sort of ruins you can see in the

photograph on the opposite page.

Naturally, in these very heavy air-raids there were many civilian casualties. In the famous and often criticised R.A.F. raid on the beautiful city of Dresden, in February 1945, as many people were killed by conventional bombs as were later to die as the result of the atomic explosion over Hiroshima. At the time however, these methods seemed the only way to break the German people's resolve to go on fighting.

1. Write a paragraph in your own words about the bomber offensive against Germany.

2. Draw the outline of the Lancaster bomber in your book.

Despite the huge scale of the bomber offensive against Germany and the large number of deaths it caused, it is now clear that its results were rather limited. German civilians tended to react to the bombing in much the same way as Londoners did during the Blitz. The Allied air-raids seem to have made them even more determined to fight on.

The ruins of Hamburg

German industry also coped very well with the bombing. By brilliant organisation, the Germans managed to increase their industrial output until the last months of the war. Only then did the bombing really begin to make a significant difference. By and large, therefore, the great area bombing raids were a failure.

The most successful air-raids of the war were probably the much smaller, more highly-specialised attacks made against specific targets. The attacks made by the Americans on the German synthetic oil plants and the ball-bearing factories had very damaging effects on the German war effort. Considerable disruption was also caused by the famous R.A.F. Dam Buster raid on May 17th 1943.

This raid, carried out by nineteen Lancasters of 617 Squadron led by Wing Commander Guy Gibson, D.S.O., D.F.C., used the famous 'bouncing bomb' designed by Barnes Wallis to breach the Moehne and Eder Dams. The Moehne Dam supplied large parts of the industrial Ruhr valley with water and hydro-electrical power, and the bombing caused extensive damage which was not finally repaired until September 1943. Albert Speer, the head of Hitler's war industry, has said that this raid came near to achieving more than all the rest of the bomber offensive put together.

3. How successful was the bomber offensive against Germany?

4. Try to find some more information about the Dam Busters, and then write a paragraph about the raid on the Moehne and Eder Dams. Draw the diagram below to illustrate your answer.

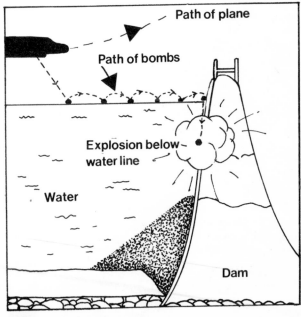

The bouncing bomb

Chapter 17 The War in the Pacific

A U.S. Marine battle headquarters in the jungle on Guadalcanal

The rapid Japanese advance, which we looked at in Chapter 6, gave Japan control of a huge Far Eastern empire, and it looked at one stage as if her armies might even sweep on and invade Australia. However, this danger was averted by the victory of the American fleet in the Battle of the Coral Sea in May 1942, and slowly the tide of the Pacific War began to turn.

The American fleet won another important victory at the Battle of Midway in June 1942, which restored the balance of naval strength in the Pacific. Now, the United States, which bore the brunt of the fighting in the Far East, was ready to go over to the offensive.

The Pacific campaign was a difficult one to fight. Because the Japanese conquests were so scattered, the only way to tackle the problem was to clear the Japanese from the ring of islands which they occupied and establish American bases on them instead. It was hoped that these island bases could be extended closer and closer to Japan itself until, eventually, U.S. forces would be in a position to threaten the Japanese mainland.

'Island hopping' was the name given to this American strategy, which began in 1943 with the capture of Guadalcanal. It continued throughout 1943 and into 1944 as the U.S. Marines occupied the Gilbert Islands, the Marshalls and the Marianas. By the late summer of 1944 the Americans were poised to attack the Philippines and fulfil the promise made by the American General MacArthur that he would return to liberate the people of those islands from Japanese control.

1. Find a map of the Pacific area in your atlas and find the groups of islands mentioned in this chapter so far.

2. Answer these questions in your own words.

What was the importance of the Battle of the Coral Sea?

What did the Battle of Midway restore?

What do you understand by the term 'island hopping'?

Which groups of islands did the United States marines capture?

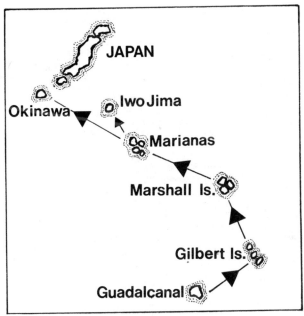

The American 'island hopping' strategy

A Japanese ceremonial sword

3. Copy the picture above, which shows how the 'island hopping' strategy in the Pacific operated.

The attack on the Philippines opened with the greatest naval engagement in history, the Battle of Leyte Gulf. This battle in which the Japanese fleet was destroyed gave the United States complete sea supremacy in the Pacific. However, they still had a stiff fight on their hands. Both in the Philippines, which fell in February 1945, and in later battles, the Japanese fought with fierce determination. The Japanese soldiers believed that surrender brought dishonour. They preferred to die for their Emperor rather than give in. The same belief inspired the Kamikaze suicide pilots who crashed their explosive-laden planes into the decks of American warships.

In the face of this sort of opposition the Americans suffered very heavy losses. The last stage of the 'island hopping' campaign, for example, which involved the capture of the two forward bases of Iwo Jima and Okinawa, brought some of the fiercest resistance and the highest American casualties of the whole Pacific war.

The capture of these two islands was however a major success for the United States. Iwo Jima,

which fell in February 1945, and Okinawa, where resistance finally came to an end in June 1945, were both within striking distance of Japan. From Okinawa it was possible for the American bombers to fly round-the-clock bombing missions against the chief Japanese cities with fighter cover from air bases on Iwo Jima. Therefore, by securing these two islands, the Americans had gained the means of ending the Pacific war.

4. Write a paragraph in your own words describing the war in the Pacific from the Battle of Leyte Gulf to the capture of Iwo Jima and Okinawa.

5. Use the reference books in your school library to find out some more information about the Battle of Leyte Gulf. How did it differ from the other great naval battles in history?

6. Above is a picture of the ceremonial sword worn by the Kamikaze suicide flyers. Draw it in your book and write one or two sentences about the Kamikaze pilots.

Chapter 18 The D-Day Landings

The troops go ashore on D-Day

On D-Day, June 6th 1944, the invasion of Hitler's Europe from the west began. An armada of nearly 4,000 ships carried in the region of 130,000 troops across the English Channel, to land on the coast of Normandy in northern France. Paratroopers, who were landed in the rear to cut the German lines of communication, helped to ensure the success of the operation. Within days of establishing the first beach-heads on D-Day itself, thousands of British, American and Canadian troops had been landed, and hundreds of tonnes of stores and equipment had been put ashore.

The task of supplying the fighting troops became easier after the capture of the port of Cherbourg on June 26th 1944. The fall of Caen on July 8th, after days of bitter fighting, gave the Allies control of Normandy and from that point onwards the break-out into the rest of France was only a matter of time.

After regrouping their forces, the Allies began to push eastwards in two main directions. The Americans moved on Paris which was liberated on August 24th 1944. They then advanced towards the French–German frontier, reinforced by additional troops who had landed in southern France on August 15th. The British, meanwhile, moved forward further north and advanced through Belgium and into Holland. Their target was the Rhine and the important German industrial towns in the Ruhr.

1. D-Day was the greatest amphibious operation ever mounted in any war. What does the term 'amphibious' mean?

2. Answer these questions in your own words.

When was D-Day?

How many ships were used in the landings?

What sort of troops were used to disrupt German communications?

Which port was captured and used to supply the invasion forces?

Which town was captured to give the Allies control of Normandy?

When the Allies broke out of the Normandy bridgehead, in which two directions did they move?

When was Paris liberated from German control?

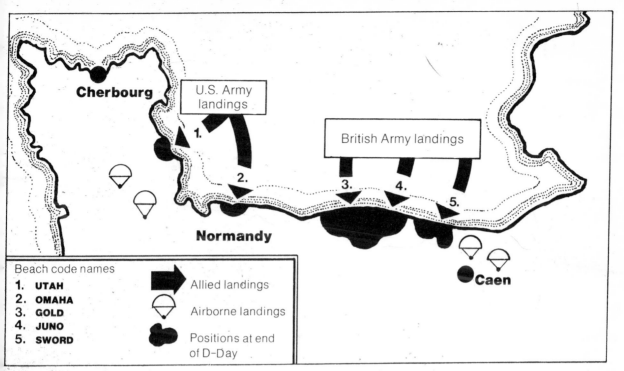

Cherbourg

U.S. Army landings

British Army landings

1.

2.

3.

4.

5.

Normandy

●**Caen**

Beach code names
1. **UTAH**
2. **OMAHA**
3. **GOLD**
4. **JUNO**
5. **SWORD**

Allied landings

Airborne landings

Positions at end
of D-Day

The D-Day landings

The D-Day landings were the biggest military operation ever attempted, and they required very careful planning and preparation. The Supreme Commander, the American General Eisenhower, and his staff were busy for months before the invasion took place. They had to arrange for the assembly of all the troops and landing craft and work out all the details of the co-operation they would need from the navy and the airforce. In addition, teams of scientists and engineers were set to work to solve the many technical problems which such an invasion involved, and they came up with some brilliant answers.

They designed, for example, a floating harbour called Mulberry, which was towed across the Channel in prefabricated sections and then anchored off the Normandy beaches. Large ships were able to tie up and unload their stores on to this harbour, even before the capture of Cherbourg gave the Allies a deep water port. Another successful scheme was PLUTO, the pipe line under the ocean which carried fuel oil on the bed of the Channel from Britain to France.

Another interesting aspect of the preparations made for the D-Day invasion was the work done by the Allied intelligence services. They made secret arrangements with the Maquis, the French resistance fighters, to blow up vital railway bridges and other targets behind the German lines. They also tricked the Germans into thinking the invasion was not going to be in Normandy at all. As a result, on the day of the landings, the defences on that part of the French coast were not as strong as they might have been.

3. Write a few sentences about the following:

Mulberry Harbour
PLUTO
The Maquis.

4. See if you can borrow a book called 'The Secrets of D-Day' by Gilles Perrault from your local library. In it you will find the full story of how the Allied intelligence services tricked the Germans into thinking the D-Day landings would be made near Calais.

5. Draw the map of the D-Day landings in your book.

6. Use the reference books in your library to try to find out some more about General Eisenhower, the Allied Supreme Commander.

Chapter 19 The V-Weapons

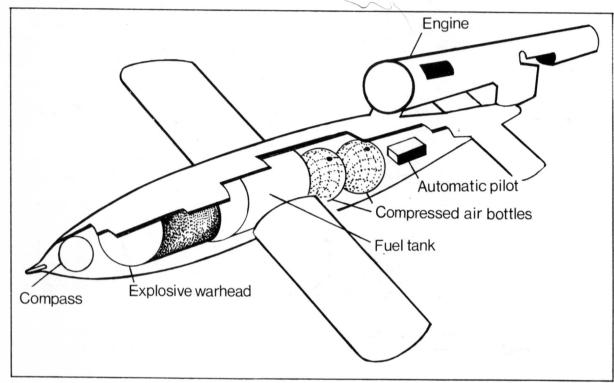

Engine

Automatic pilot

Compressed air bottles

Fuel tank

Compass

Explosive warhead

The V.1 flying bomb

Early in 1943 news reached London via agents of the Polish underground movement that the Germans had built a secret experimental station at Peenemünde on the Baltic to test pilotless aircraft and rocket bombs. R.A.F. reconnaissance planes confirmed this information with aerial photographs in May 1943, and in August a bombing raid by the R.A.F. severely damaged the Peenemünde site and put back development work by several months.

However, the R.A.F. could not halt the work on the two projects altogether. Hitler had given the development of the pilotless jet-propelled V.1 and the rocket-powered V.2 his full backing. These were to be his *Vergeltungswaffen* or 'weapons of revenge', which he planned to use to turn the tide of the war in his favour. By February 1944 ninety-six launching sites for the V.1 had been built by the Germans in northern France, and although the R.A.F. and the U.S.A.F. destroyed seventy-three of them it was obvious that Britain was to be subjected once again to a bombardment from the air of a new and rather terrible kind. 'Push-button' warfare had arrived, and this country was to feel its first effects.

1. Answer these questions in your own words.

What was the V.1?

What was the V.2?

How did the V-weapons get their names?

Where were they developed by the Germans?

How did the British first learn of their development?

What put back the German experimental work on the V-weapons for several months?

How many launching sites did the Germans build for their planned bombardment of Britain?

How many of these sites were destroyed by the R.A.F. and the U.S.A.F.?

An unexploded V.1

2. Draw the picture of the V.1 flying bomb opposite. Label all the parts.

The young German scientist, Wernher von Braun, and his team of experts, who developed the revenge weapons, had the V.1 ready for operational use by the summer of 1944. The first flying bomb was launched on June 13th, just one week after D-Day. The V.1, carrying one tonne of high-explosive and travelling at a speed of 640 kilometres per hour, was given just enough fuel to carry it to its target, at which point the engine cut out and it fell from the sky.

In all, the Germans launched about 8,000 V.1s, London being the chief target. However, they did not have the effect Hitler had hoped for. The Londoners, who christened them 'Buzzbombs' and 'Doodle-bugs', grew used to the V.1s and learned that they only had to run for cover when they heard the engine cut out.

The V.2s were rather more successful. These forerunners of the modern moon rockets also carried about one tonne of high-explosive, but they plunged to the earth after rising to a height of over a hundred kilometres. They gave no warning of their approach, and they might have succeeded in spreading considerably more terror than the V.1s if more of them had been fired.

Fortunately, only about 1,000 V.2s fell on Britain before their launching sites, along with those of the V.1 flying bombs, were overrun by the advancing Allied armies. The revenge weapons upon which Hitler and the German people had pinned such hopes were largely a failure.

3. Write a paragraph in your own words about the V-weapons and the part they played in the Second World War.

4. At the end of the war von Braun was captured by the Americans and he began to work on their rocket programme. Von Braun's skill and knowledge played an important part in putting the first man on the moon. See if you can find out some more about the career of this famous scientist.

5. See if you can find a picture of a V.2 rocket in the Second World War section of your school library and draw one in your book.

6. Use your atlas to find out where Peenemünde is.

Chapter 20 The Defeat of Germany

The Allied advance in 1945

By the beginning of 1945 it was obvious that Germany had lost the war. The Russians were pressing in from the east, the British and Americans were advancing from the west and the German troops doggedly defending Italy knew that they must expect a new Allied attack from the south. Round-the-clock bombing raids were systematically destroying Germany's ability to supply her armies with the weapons which they needed to continue the struggle. At this point it would have been sensible for the Germans to have given in and asked for peace.

Unfortunately, this was not really possible. Churchill, Stalin and Roosevelt, the Allied leaders, had publicly stated that Germany could expect no terms. The only way the war could end was for the Nazi leaders to surrender unconditionally, and this they were not prepared to do. With nothing to gain from giving in, the Germans felt compelled to go on fighting. Old men and children were called up to serve their country, and they did so with remarkable courage, even when they must have known that all was lost.

Joseph Goebbels, Hitler's propaganda minister, played an important part in sustaining public morale by visiting bombed cities and making inspiring speeches and radio broadcasts to the German people. His influence, coupled with their desperate fear of the Russian invaders made the Germans determined to struggle on to the very end. The closing months of the war saw some of the most bitter fighting of the whole conflict.

1. Draw the diagram on the opposite page in your book, and then write a few sentences in your own words about the dangers which Germany faced.

2. Explain the meaning of the term 'unconditional surrender'.

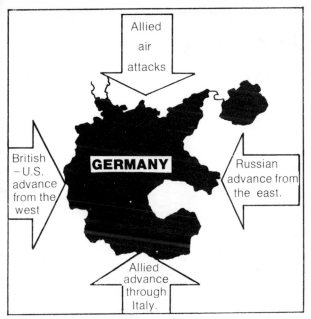

The defeat of Germany

Hitler with his chiefs of staff

The bravery and military skill demonstrated by the Germans in the closing months of the war could do no more than delay the final outcome, however. Defeat was inevitable. In March 1945 the British and Americans under General Eisenhower crossed the Rhine and began to advance through German territory, while the Russians, pouring in from the east, began their final push towards Berlin.

The bombing campaign built up to a final pitch of intensity. In many German cities people were camping among the ruins of their former homes without light, heat or water, and were forced to scavenge amongst the rubble for food, like animals. In many areas normal life had completely broken down.

Hitler, in these closing weeks of the war, was a physical and mental wreck. The Bomb Plot of July 1944, in which he had only narrowly escaped death, had left him with a partly-paralysed arm and a nervous twitch in his face. The more serious the news became, the more his mind manufactured impossible answers to his problems. As he sat plotting the movements of non-existent armies on the map in his underground *Führerbunker* in the middle of Berlin, Hitler lost all touch with reality.

In April 1945, with Russian tanks already rumbling through the outskirts of Berlin, and with the centre of the city under constant shellfire, even Hitler's closest colleagues began to desert him. Slipping out of the bunker in ones or twos, they made their escape from Berlin before it was completely surrounded, leaving the Führer to his fate.

Only the faithful Goebbels and his wife, Martin Bormann and Hitler's mistress, Eva Braun, stayed with him. Finally, when all was lost, in the early hours of April 29th 1945, Hitler married Eva Braun, and twenty-four hours later he and his new bride committed suicide. So, too, did Joseph and Magda Goebbels after they had poisoned their six children.

With the Führer gone, it only remained for Germany to make peace with the Allies. Grand Admiral Doenitz, who had been named by Hitler as his successor, contacted the Allies and asked for peace. The war in Europe came to an end at midnight on May 8th 1945. Hitler's Third Reich, which he had boasted would last a thousand years, had outlived him by just one week.

3. Write a paragraph in your own words about the closing weeks of the war and Hitler's death in the 'Führerbunker' in Berlin on April 30th 1945.

4. In Britain May 8th 1945 was celebrated as V.E. Day, which stood for Victory in Europe. Ask those members of your family who remember it how they celebrated that day.

45

Chapter 21 Victory in the Pacific

When Germany surrendered in May 1945, Japan was also close to defeat. The American 'island hopping' strategy had carried them to Iwo Jima and Okinawa, only 1,290 kilometres south of Japan, and British forces in Burma had almost cleared that country of the Japanese invaders.

The long struggle in Burma by the 'forgotten army' of British and Indian troops attracted only a small amount of attention at the time. Yet it was a bitter campaign, fought through monsoon rains and difficult jungle country. The battle had been as much against diseases such as malaria and dysentery as against the Japanese. However, it was brought to a triumphant conclusion in May 1945 when British troops re-occupied Rangoon. It was apparent that a final blow could force Japan out of the war altogether.

The question was how this blow should be delivered. It was now quite possible to mount a full-scale invasion of the Japanese mainland. However, the way in which Japan's soldiers had resisted the Americans on Iwo Jima and Okinawa had demonstrated what a costly operation a landing on Japan would be. Military experts estimated that it might claim more casualties than all the rest of the Pacific fighting.

President Truman, the American leader who had taken over only a few months before, when President Roosevelt died, was faced with a difficult decision. The atomic bomb had been developed by this time, and Truman knew that by using it he could probably bring the war to a speedy conclusion. He decided that, in order to save American lives, he was justified in using this new and most terrible of all weapons.

1. Answer these questions in your own words.

How close was Japan to defeat when the war in Europe ended?

Which area of the Far East was cleared of Japanese soldiers by British and Indian troops?

In which two ways could Japan have been defeated in 1945?

Why did President Truman choose the alternative of dropping the atomic bomb?

An atomic explosion

The atomic bomb was developed in the United States by a team of American and British scientists working in great secrecy on a huge research project which cost millions of dollars. The first test explosion took place on July 17th 1945 in the New Mexico desert and an operational bomb was ready for use against Japan early in August.

The city of Hiroshima was chosen as the first target, and the bomb was dropped on August 6th 1945. It was released by parachute from a U.S.A.F. Flying Fortress and exploded at a height of about 600 metres above the city.

(Above right) Hiroshima after the bomb
(Below right) Where the bombs fell

The heat of the terrible explosion caused a fire-storm which destroyed more than half the city and killed 80,000 people. Almost the same number suffered injury from the blast and from radiation burns. Three days later, on August 9th 1945, a second atomic bomb was dropped on Nagasaki which caused similar damage and killed 40,000 people. The following day Japan asked for peace.

The formal Japanese surrender was made on September 2nd 1945, when General MacArthur, who had so brilliantly organised the American army's Pacific campaign, received the Japanese envoys on board the U.S. battleship *Missouri* in Tokyo Bay. With this surrender the Second World War came to an end. The conflict had lasted for six years and had been truly world-wide. It had caused millions of deaths and untold human suffering, as well as material damage, and it left behind some terrible problems.

After Hiroshima and Nagasaki, the world's statesmen were well aware of what the consequences would be if they failed to resolve these problems and to prevent future world-wide conflict. The nuclear age dawned in August 1945 and it became all too obvious that a future war on the scale of the 1939–45 conflict could mean the end of human civilisation. The leaders of all the world's nations now had the fearful responsibility of trying to ensure that there should never be a Third World War.

2. Write a paragraph in your own words about the use of the atomic bomb in 1945 and then draw the map at the bottom of this page.

3. Many people think that the atomic bomb should never have been used in any circumstances. Write a paragraph to say whether you agree or disagree with this point of view.

4. Write two or three sentences saying whether you think there will ever be a Third World War and giving your reasons. Which do you think are likely to be the major powers involved, if there is?

Hiroshima Aug. 6th 1945

Nagasaki Aug. 9th 1945

JAPAN

Tokyo

Hiroshima

Nagasaki

To the teacher

The last four books in the *Knowing British History* series follow the same general format as earlier titles, but the subject matter has been chosen for its relevance to the slightly older pupils who generally study modern history. Follow-up reading and research have been emphasised, and it is expected that teachers will wish to set additional exercises and to use other reference material, including films, television and radio broadcasts. It is also hoped that, in addition to the pupil's own exercise book or scrapbook, the follow-up work may take the form of imaginative work in art and written English, and the preparation of displays. Much local research is also possible on historical events as recent as those covered in the four books, and a great deal of interesting material can be obtained if pupils are encouraged to interview neighbours and members of their own families on audio or video tape recorders.

Most teachers will wish to add to the information contained in *The Second World War*, using the enormous amount of material available in the form of books, films, filmstrips and so on. Because so much has been published on the war, great care must be exercised in how this is used in the classroom. Detailed military history can be very confusing to pupils whose background knowledge of the war is limited, and it is suggested that teachers should select their own extracts from the many first-hand accounts of the fighting, in order to give their classes something of the feel of, for instance, sailing in an Arctic convoy, or trying to keep a bomber steady as it runs in over a target.

Suggestions have been made in the preceding chapters concerning the collection of wartime memories. It is hoped that research of this type, undertaken by the pupils themselves, will form a large part of the follow-up work to individual chapters. Family reminiscences about the Blitz, food rationing, or being an evacuee, can be collected in a class scrapbook to make very interesting reading. Such memories can also give a lively and often local flavour to display work when combined with old ration books, gas masks, medals and other relics of the war which pupils can usually collect quite easily.

Finally, the attention of the teacher is directed to the excellent collection of wartime relics in the Imperial War Museum in London. If it is possible to take classes to the Museum, any problems of stimulating interest in the war will be solved.